History for Kids: The Illustrated Lives of A..........   ci

By Charles River Editors

A statue of Archimedes in Berlin

About Charles River Editors

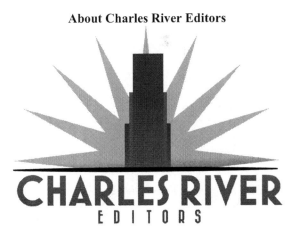

Charles River Editors was founded by Harvard and MIT alumni to provide superior editing and original writing services, with the expertise to create digital content for publishers across a vast range of subject matter. In addition to providing original digital content for third party publishers, Charles River Editors republishes civilization's greatest literary works, bringing them to a new generation via ebooks.

Introduction

***Archimedes Thoughtful*, a 1620 painting by Domenico Fetti**

Archimedes (circa 287-212 ~~A.D.~~) B.C.

"Give me a place to stand, and I shall move the world.'"– Archimedes

In Charles River Editors' History for Kids series, your children can learn about history's most important people and events in an easy, entertaining, and educational way. Pictures help bring the story to life, and the concise but comprehensive book will keep your kid's attention all the way to the end.

Over 1500 years before Leonardo Da Vinci became the Renaissance Man, antiquity had its own in the form of Archimedes, one of the most famous Ancient Greeks. An engineer, mathematician, physicist, scientist and astronomer all rolled into one, Archimedes has been credited for making groundbreaking discoveries, some of which are undoubtedly fact and others that are almost certainly myth. Regardless, he's considered the first man to determine a way to measure an object's mass, and also the first man to realize that refracting the Sun's light could burn something, theorizing the existence of lasers over two millennia before they existed. People still use the design of the Archimedes screw in water pumps today, and modern scholars have tried to link him to the recently discovered Antikythera mechanism, an ancient "computer" of sorts that used mechanics to accurately chart astronomical data depending on the date it was set to.

Archimedes was a legend even among the Romans, who were expanding their empire during the great scientist's own lifetime. A Roman soldier has long been blamed for killing Archimedes after taking over Syracuse, but not before Archimedes reportedly helped the island's defenses with ingenious devices that burned Roman ships and even lifted some of them out of the water. The stories are probably apocryphal, but they speak to the man's reputation even among his contemporaries, and Cicero himself went to visit Archimedes' tomb.

It has long been difficult to separate fact from legend in the story of Archimedes' life, from his death to his legendary discovery of how to differentiate gold from fool's gold, but many of his works survived antiquity, and many others were quoted by other ancient writers. As a result, even while his life and death remain topics of debate, his writings and measurements are factually established and well known, and they range on everything from measuring an object's density to measuring circles and parabolas.

History for Kids: The Illustrated Lives of Archimedes and Leonardo Da Vinci chronicles the life, stories, and legacy of the famous Greek mathematician and scientist. Along with pictures of depicting important people and places, as well as a Table of Contents, your kids will learn about Archimedes like never before.

Leonardo made this picture of himself around 1512

Leonardo Da Vinci (1452-1519)

"Iron rusts from disuse; stagnant water loses its purity and in cold weather becomes frozen; even so does inaction sap the vigor of the mind." – Leonardo

In Charles River Editors' History for Kids series, your children can learn about history's most important people and events in an easy, entertaining, and educational way. Pictures help bring the story to life, and the concise but comprehensive book will keep your kid's attention all the way to the end.

The Renaissance spawned the use of the label "Renaissance Man" to describe a person who is extremely talented in multiple fields, and no discussion of the Renaissance is complete without the original "Renaissance Man", Leonardo da Vinci. Indeed, if 100 people are asked to describe Leonardo in one word, they might give 100 answers. As the world's most famous polymath and genius, Leonardo found time to be a painter, sculptor, architect, musician, scientist, mathematician, engineer, inventor, anatomist, geologist, cartographer, botanist, and writer.

It would be hard to determine which field Leonardo had the greatest influence in. His "Mona Lisa" and "The Last Supper" are among the most famous paintings of all time, standing up against even Michelangelo's work. But even if he was not the age's greatest artist, Leonardo may have conducted his most influential work was done in other fields. His emphasis on the importance of Nature would influence Enlightened philosophers centuries later, and he sketched speculative designs for gadgets like helicopters that would take another 4 centuries to create. Leonardo's vision and philosophy were made possible by his astounding work as a mathematician, engineer and scientist. At a time when much of science was dictated by Church teachings, Leonardo studied geology and anatomy long before they truly even became scientific fields, and he used his incredible artistic abilities to sketch the famous Vitruvian Man, linking art and science together.

Leonardo also conducted scientific experiments using empirical methods nearly 150 years before Rene Descartes' "Discourse on Method." As Leonardo explained in his writings, "Many will think they may reasonably blame me by alleging that my proofs are opposed to the authority of certain men held in the highest reverence by their inexperienced judgments; not considering that my works are the issue of pure and simple experience, who is the one true mistress."

History for Kids: The Illustrated Lives of Archimedes and Leonardo Da Vinci chronicles Leonardo's amazing life and work. Along with pictures of important people, places, and events in his life, your kids will learn about Leonardo like never before.

Archimedes

Chapter 1: Who Was Archimedes?

Archimedes was one of the most important people in the ancient world. He did a lot of work in science and math that we still use today. People have loved him for over 2,000 years too. The state of California used one of Archimedes' quotes as its own state quote! A lot of people think Archimedes was like Leonardo Da Vinci. Both men worked on a lot of different things. They also worked on weapons. Archimedes wanted to protect his home from the Romans.

Archimedes lived over 2,000 years ago, but we still have a lot of what he wrote. It was found in the 1840s by a religious man. He went to Constantinople, Turkey to find religious works. He found an old text that had been written over by someone else. Someone had written over Archimedes' math equations! Over 10 of Archimedes' works still exist today.

Archimedes has always been famous. But that doesn't mean we know a lot about him. Ancient writers wrote a lot of stories about him. Sometimes it's hard to tell if they're true or not. Ancient Greece was no long as strong when Archimedes was alive. That means there weren't many Greek historians. A Roman historian named Polybius wrote a little about Archimedes. But Polybius was writing about Rome's wars. He didn't write a biography of Archimedes. He wrote about how Archimedes fought the Romans. Other historians like Livy and Plutarch wrote about Archimedes too. But they used what they read from Polybius. Nobody who lived with Archimedes wrote about him. Today, people are still trying to learn more about him.

A Roman sculpture of the historian Polybius

An old picture someone drew of the historian Livy.

A statue of Plutarch

A statue of Archimedes

Archimedes was born around 285 B.C. in the city of Syracuse. Syracuse was on the island of Sicily, which is by Italy. Even though it was close to Rome, Syracuse was not Roman. It had been a Greek city-state for a long time. It was also very strong. People in Carthage tried to take over Syracuse and couldn't. Athens tried to take it before Archimedes was born and couldn't take it either.

Syracuse was still fighting Carthage when Archimedes was born. Nobody knows who his parents were. Some people think his father Phidias was an astronomer. This might be why Archimedes liked science. Archimedes might also have been a relative of a man named Hiero. In 275, Hiero became King of Syracuse. Archimedes was a teenager back then. Some people think that King Hiero helped Archimedes learn.

Historians think that Archimedes went to Alexandria, Egypt as a young boy. Alexandria had a famous library then. It was the best place for students to learn about math and science. Some of Archimedes' work talks about his friends. They were called Conon of Samos and Eratosthenes of Cyrene. Conon worked on astronomy and math. Eratosthenes worked on geography. Eratosthenes even invented the word geography! Eratosthenes was able to figure out how large the Earth was by looking at shadows during the day.

Someone drew a picture of what they thought Eratosthenes looked like.

At some point, Archimedes went back home to Syracuse. It's hard to tell how long he was in Alexandria. But today people think he started writing soon after he came home to Syracuse. This is because Hiero was still the King of Syracuse.

One of Archimedes' friends wrote about him. His friend's name was Heracleides. But

Heracleides' book was lost. This means nobody knows if Archimedes was married or had kids. But we do know that Archimedes spent most of his time on his work. King Hiero let Archimedes do all the work he wanted. It seems Archimedes didn't have to worry about money. Hiero may have even asked Archimedes to do the work for him. He needed all the help he could get against Carthage and Rome.

King Hiero died in 215 B.C. Archimedes was probably around 70 years old then. But Archimedes was still working hard. The next ruler of Syracuse was named Hieronymus. Hieronymus thought Carthage was going to destroy Rome. He decided to help Carthage fight. However, Rome ended up beating Carthage. The Romans wanted to destroy Hieronymus and Syracuse too.

In 214 B.C., the Romans sent an army and navy to Syracuse. Their boats surrounded Syracuse's boats and their ports. The Roman army also surrounded the city of Syracuse. They wanted Syracuse to give up fighting.

Syracuse kept fighting for two years. Roman writers said this is because Archimedes helped them. They said Archimedes made a "Mirror" and a "Claw". The mirror bounced the sun's rays onto Roman boats and burned them. The claw could pick up Roman ships out of the water! However, the Romans eventually were able to get into the city of Syracuse. A small group climbed over Syracuse's walls and opened the gates for other Roman soldiers.

The Roman soldiers started killing people in Syracuse. But the Roman general didn't want his men to kill Archimedes. The general's name was Marcellus. He told his men to capture Archimedes alive. Roman soldiers found Archimedes at his home working. One story said that a Roman soldier tried to pull him away from his work. Then Archimedes shouted, "Do not disturb my circles!" This made the soldiers so mad that he killed Archimedes. Another story said Archimedes tried to surrender. But then the Romans thought he had a weapon. It's not clear how Archimedes was killed. But he did not survive the Roman attack.

Chapter 2: Inventions

The Romans knew Archimedes made new kinds of weapons. That might be why the Roman general wanted his soldiers to take Archimedes alive. Some people think the Romans wanted to use Archimedes and his weapons. Of course, Archimedes made a lot of other things too. Here are some of the things Archimedes made.

Archimedes Claw*:* Ancient Roman writers talked a lot about a weapon Archimedes made. Today it is called the Claw. Back then, people called it "The Ship-Shaker", "The Snatcher", and the "Iron Hand". Nobody is sure what the Claw looked like. The Romans didn't try to make one either. Some people don't think the Claw existed.

However, scientists think that the Claw did exist. People have been able to make the Claw today. The Claw was probably like a very big crane. It used men or oxen to pull the Claw. The people in Syracuse used it to lift Roman ships out of the water. This made the Roman ships sink. This made sure the Roman ships didn't get into Syracuse's port.

Giulio Parigi's painting of the Claw

Archimedes Mirror: A Roman named Lucian wrote about Archimedes using mirrors to burn Roman ships. He wrote 300 years after Archimedes died. People still argue about whether Archimedes really used the mirrors. Another Greek named Anthemius wrote about using mirrors in 400 A.D. That was 600 years after Archimedes died.

Anthemius and Lucian wrote that Archimedes made a heat ray out of mirrors. They said Archimedes had sunlight bounce off the mirrors and burn Roman ships. People still try to use mirrors to create the heat ray today. A show called *Mythbusters* tried to do it just a few years ago.

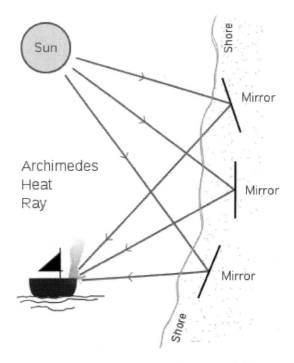

Archimedes probably used bronze mirrors. He would have needed them to be able to spin around too. If the mirrors all bounced sunlight onto the same spot, they could make wood burn. It could be as hot as 570 degrees! Some ships would just start burning and the Romans didn't know why. It would have been very scary to be on the ships. The light would also blind the Roman sailors. That would make it harder to sail.

There's another reason people don't think Archimedes used mirrors. This is because Syracuse could have used fire arrows and other things. They might not have needed mirrors.

Archimedes Screw: Archimedes is very famous for other inventions too. We still use some of them today. The Archimedes Screw was a tool that could lift water up from the shore. People didn't really know how to do it back then. The Romans used aqueducts or carried buckets that had wheels on them.

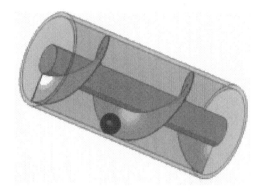

Archimedes Screw

The Archimedes Screw was shaped like a cylinder. He might have made it out of wood or metal. He could place the bottom part of the screw in the water. Then he would turn the screw. It would move the water up to the top of the screw. The screw would only leak a little water.

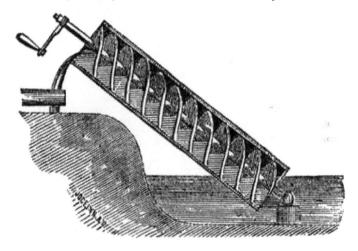

Illustration of the Screw

The Screw helped the people of Syracuse. The Romans liked it so much that they used it too. People could use it to bring water to their farms back then. People still use it today. The Netherlands uses it to make water go down instead of up.

Archimedes Lever and Planetarium: Archimedes's most famous quote is "Give me a place to stand and I shall move the world." This quote was about using a lever. Archimedes wasn't the first to use a lever. But he discovered a lot of important things by using them. He was able to use the lever for ropes and pulleys. This made carrying things much easier. Archimedes also realized that men could lift something far easier with levers. They could lift very heavy objects too. That's why Archimedes said he could even move the whole Earth with a lever.

A drawing of Archimedes using a lever with the world on it

Archimedes also made a Planetarium. The Romans were amazed by it. Roman writers wrote all about it. For 2,000 years, people didn't know if it actually existed. But then a Planetarium was found on an ancient ship at the bottom of a sea. It had sunk with one of them on the ship.

The planetarium showed the Earth, the Sun, and the Moon. When people would spin the Earth, it would also make the Sun and Moon orbit around it. People could track where the Sun and Moon would appear in the sky as the Earth moved. It showed just how much Archimedes knew about astronomy. It also showed how good Archimedes was with mechanics. An Egyptian writer said that Archimedes even wrote a paper about how to make a planetarium. The Romans took two of Archimedes's planetariums back to Rome. They even put one in a temple. That's how impressed they were.

The Romans used a lot of Archimedes' inventions. They also took them to other lands that they conquered. This meant that Archimedes's work spread all across the Roman Empire. People all over the world were using his things.

Chapter 3: Theories

Archimedes made a lot of things. But he also wrote a lot of theories. This was back before people knew a lot about math. People didn't even know what the study of physics was then either. Algebra wasn't taught to people. This means Archimedes learned it all on his own.

One of the most important things Archimedes found out was how to figure out an object's density. It also led to the most famous moment of his life. The King of Syracuse bought a special gold crown. He wanted to give it to one of the temples. But the King didn't trust goldsmiths. He thought they would use fool's gold and trick him.

The King didn't know how to tell if the crown was made of gold or not. He asked Archimedes to help. Archimedes had to make a new way to solve the problem because he couldn't break the crown.

Archimedes worked a long time trying to figure it out. He was stumped. But then he got ready to take a bath. When he got in the tub, he saw that the water would rise as he got in. Now he knew he could use water levels to find out if the crown was made of gold. Ancient writers say that Archimedes was so happy that he ran out of his house and shouted "Eureka!". Eureka was Greek for "I have it!" Archimedes was so excited that he even forgot to put his clothes on!

Archimedes was able to find out the crown was made of real gold. He put the crown in water and found out how much the water rose. Then he found a bar of gold that weighed the same as the crown. When he put that in the water, the water rose just as high. This meant the crown was made out of pure gold. King Hiero could then give the crown to the temple.

Some people don't believe that story though. They actually think Archimedes had figured it out before. This is because Archimedes may have already written a work called *On Floating Bodies*. Archimedes had found out that a solid object would push up some water as it went into the water. If a 10 pound object sank in the water, it made 10 pounds of water rise. But if a 10 pound object floated, it made less than 10 pounds of water rise. This is how people could find out if something would float.

If Archimedes already knew this, he could figure out if the crown was made of gold right away. He could have put the crown on one side of a scale and a gold bar on the other. Then he could put the scale in the water. Both objects pushed the same amount of water up. That's how Archimedes knew the crown was pure gold.

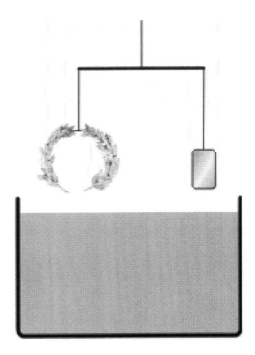

Nobody knows for sure which story is true. But either way, Archimedes made an important discovery.

Archimedes also did a lot of math work. He could only make a theory by finding out that other theories weren't true. Nobody had come up with the proof system yet.

Archimedes probably wrote about how he found out math theories. But those works were lost. People no longer know how he figured out what he did. The good news is that we know the results.

Archimedes was able to figure out the square root of the number 3. That's something that people would use a calculator for today.

Archimedes wrote a lot about circles. Some of those works are still read today. Archimedes could also find out the area of a circle. He did this with right angle triangles. He made sure one of the triangle's sides was the same length as the circle's radius. Then he made sure the biggest side of the triangle was the same length of the circle's circumference. This would make the area of the triangle and the circle the same.

Archimedes was also able to figure out the ratio between a circle's circumference and diameter. He wrote that the ratio was about 3.15 to 1. He was very accurate. Today the ratio is known as Pi (π).

How did Archimedes figure it out? He drew a circle inside a hexagon. Then he drew a smaller hexagon inside the circle. Then he doubled the sides of each hexagon. Archimedes then used the Pythagoras Theory to figure out the length of the new objects. Archimedes even found out that the area of a circle was equal to Pi times the radius squared. Kids still learn about this in geometry classes today. Only a few Greeks even knew what geometry was back then.

Archimedes was able to put his work to good use. Archimedes wrote a work called *Sand Reckoner*. He was trying to figure out how many grains of sand would cover the whole world! He used math to come up with a huge number. He also tried to find out how big the universe was. When Archimedes was working on that, he said that the Earth went around the Sun. Back then, people thought everything went around the Earth. Nicolaus Copernicus finally got people to know that the Earth goes around the Sun. Archimedes thought that over 1500 years before Copernicus was born!

Chapter 4: Writing

We are lucky that some of Archimedes's works are still with us. But we also know that at least 7 of his works were lost. That's because other writers talked about them. Some of the works were about spheres and other shapes.

Archimedes wrote a lot about geometry. He figured out the area of a sphere and the volume of a ball. He was the first person to figure out the surface area of a cylinder. He figured it out using levers. We still use his measurements today.

One of Archimedes's works is called the *Cattle Problem*. It's a short poem Archimedes wrote to his friend Erathosthenes. Archimedes asked his friend to try to find out the number of cattle in the herds of the sun god Apollo. He made a very hard math problem. Then he asked his friend to solve it. Nobody knows if Erathosthenes tried to solve the problem. It took 100 years before another person got the right answer.

Archimedes also made a very famous puzzle. It was called "war of the bones". It was a popular game back then. Archimedes used it to do math too. He put the puzzle in one of his works. It was only found again in the 1800s. Archimedes been dead for over 2,000 years!

Archimedes's puzzle

Archimedes may have been history's first genius. It's easy to see why. He came up with important math theories. He knew a lot about astronomy. He figured out how and why things floated. He learned these things even before most people worked on them.

Leonardo Da Vinci

Chapter 1: Early Years

Leonardo's childhood home

On April 15, 1452, Leonardo was born around Vinci, Italy. His dad was Ser Piero. His mom was a young woman named Caterina. Leonardo's dad had a lot of money. But then Caterina married another man and moved.

Leonardo stayed with his dad's family. His dad also got married again. As a little boy, Leonardo was cared for by his dad, stepmother, and grandparents. He didn't have any brothers or sisters until he was much older.

Leonardo didn't go to school. His stepmother taught him at home. So did his grandmother. He learned reading, writing, and math. Leonardo tried to learn Latin and Greek too. He didn't do a very good job with Latin or Greek though. He had to read classic books in Italian.

Leonardo read a lot. One man named Vasari wrote about Leonardo's life. He said that Leonardo knew math better than his teachers. But Leonardo also liked to draw. He was very good at art too.

Leonardo and his family moved to Florence, Italy when he was a teenager. This was in the 1460s. Florence was a very important city. That's where the Renaissance started. Florence was run by Lorenzo de Medici. He loved art. He paid artists like Michelangelo to make paintings. Lorenzo's grandfather was named Cosimo de Medici. Cosimo also loved art. He paid Donatello to make paintings.

Lorenzo de Medici

15 year old Leonardo became an apprentice to an artist in Florence. The artist's name was known as Verrocchio. Verrocchio was a well-known artist in Florence. He had a workshop for young artists. This is where Leonardo would study.

Leonardo's earliest drawing. It's a 1473 drawing of the Arno Valley. Leonardo was only 21.

Verrocchio also had a lot of musical instruments. Leonardo also got to play them too. Leonardo got to do more stuff as he got older. He could actually work on art with Verrochio. Verrochio made a painting of Jesus and an angel. Art students think Leonardo made the angel. Leonardo learned how to sculpt and paint. He also learned how to make jewelry. He even learned about guns and cannons too.

The Baptism of Christ was painted from 1472–1475 by Verrocchio and Leonardo

Verrocchio also made sculptures. He made a statue of David from the Bible from 1473-1475. Verrocchio may have used Leonardo to make the statue.

Leonardo was done being an apprentice in 1476. He stayed in Florence after that. But a lot of his art was lost. Leonardo would also start a lot of art and not finish. He always stayed busy. He was also interested in a lot of things. He didn't like to spend too much time on one thing. One of his paintings was supposed to go in an altar. It was called "The Adoration of the Magi". He didn't finish it

The Adoration of the Magi

Historians think that Leonardo worked on more than art in Florence. They think he studied animals. They also think he started making designs of weapons. But a lot of people didn't like Leonardo. They didn't like that he failed to finish his art. He was also accused of a crime. But Lorenzo de Medici liked Leonardo. He had Leonardo work on some sculptures. Leonardo said that the "Medici created me." He was also very nice to animals. He would buy birds at the market and let them fly away. He usually ate vegetables and not meat.

Chapter 2: Milan

In 1482 or 1483, Leonardo wanted to go to Milan. He wrote to the people who ruled Milan. The Duke of Milan was Ludovico Sforza. He wanted Milan to be as great as Florence. He needed good artists.

Ludovico Sforza

Leonardo didn't write to Ludovico about art though. He told Ludovico that he was working on weapons. Ludovico had to fight a lot of battles in Italy. Leonardo thought he could help. He had been drawing all kinds of weapons that had never been made. He came up with things that looked like poison gas and tanks!

Leonardo also told Ludovico that he was a good sculptor and painter. He said he could make statues "in marble, bronze and clay." He even said he could paint "as well as anyone else". Ludovico wanted to make a sculpture of a horse. He wanted a good sculptor. Ludovico also liked Leonardo because of Lorenzo de Medici. He wanted to be friends with Lorenzo. Being nice to Leonardo would help.

Ludovico told Leonardo to come to Milan. Leonardo would live there for 17 years. Ludovico wanted Leonardo for his art. Even though Leonardo didn't finish much in Florence, people liked his art. Leonardo also could play music and sing. Ludovico had Leonardo play in big festivals.

Leonardo's first work in Milan was called The Virgin of the Rocks. It is a painting that people go see in France today. It shows St. John the Baptist and the Virgin Mary with the baby Jesus.

The Virgin of the Rocks was very unique. Leonardo used a lot of triangles. It also uses darker colors than a lot of religious art.

The Virgin of the Rocks

In the 1480s, Leonardo also painted Portrait of a Musician and Lady with an Ermine. These were smaller paintings. They didn't take as much time to make.

Portrait of a Musician

A lot of people got sick in Milan in 1484 and 1485. 50,000 people died. Nobody knew why so many people were getting sick. But Leonardo thought it was because too many people lived close to each other. He was right. He drew a new design for the whole city of Milan! He wanted new roads. This would keep people away from horses and carriages. He also wanted canals to get rid of sewage. Leonardo thought Milan should be 10 small cities instead of 1 big city. Ludovico didn't follow Leonardo's plans though.

Milan was making a new cathedral from 1487-1490. Leonardo worked on it. He made drawings for what the dome would look like. Leonardo also made a wooden model of the building. But he didn't finish his work. Other people finished it. But Leonardo learned a lot about architecture.

Leonardo went to the library and even a school near Milan. He learned about the human body and animal bodies. He also started working on the horse statue Ludovico wanted. Leonardo studied horses and drew a lot of them. He even watched dead horses get dissected! Leonardo wanted the horse statue to be 20 feet tall and weigh 20,000 pounds! But he never made the statue.

Leonardo's drawing of the horse statue.

Leonardo had a lot of money now. He had a very nice house. He had horses and servants too. He also let friends live with him. One of his best friends was known as Salai. Salai said Leonardo was "like an excellent father to me." When Leonardo died, he gave the Mona Lisa to Salai.

Leonardo was spending a lot of money. This meant he needed to make a lot of money too. Leonardo had to ask Ludovico for money all the time. Ludovico didn't have it though. He spent a lot of money on war. One time he gave Leonardo more land instead of money.

Salai

Leonardo was very popular in Milan. People liked his work. They also thought he was very good looking. He was an athletic man with long hair and a beard. He also wore clothes that had a lot of bright colors. Salai said Leonardo was very strong and very nice too. Salai wrote that Leonardo "fed all his friends, rich or poor."

Leonardo began working on the greatest art of his early career in 1495. He made a very famous painting called The Last Supper. He made it for Ludovico. He wanted to look at the painting while he ate.

The Last Supper

People have studied Leonardo's painting for hundreds of years. They look for hidden things in the painting. This might be because Leonardo hadn't made a lot of paintings like The Last Supper before. The painting also had a lot of damage done to it. It doesn't look as good as it used to anymore.

Chapter 3: Notebooks

Leonardo was always thinking about a lot of things. He wrote down his ideas in notebooks. He kept notebooks for different subjects. The oldest notebook was made in the 1470s. Some of his notebooks were lost. But we still have 5,000 pages of his notebooks.

Leonardo's notebooks are amazing. He wrote them so that they could only be read in front of a mirror. When the notebooks got very big, he would put them together. He had notebooks about architecture, painting, human bodies, animal bodies, vision, science, mechanics, and math.

Leonardo's notebooks had designs and ideas that nobody else had ever made. He had flying machines in his notebooks. Nobody would fly until 1903. He also drew churches, canals, and forts. He also figured out that light moves in waves.

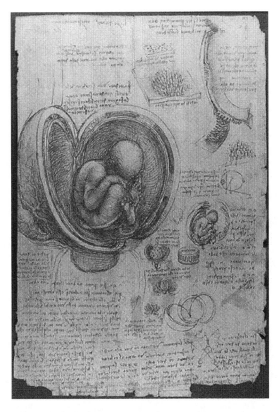

A page from Leonardo's Notebooks. It shows a baby in a mother's womb.

Leonardo loved to draw the human body. He knew more about muscles and organs than most people. He even wanted to make a book about the human body. He was one of the first people to draw muscles. One of his most famous drawings is called the Vitruvian Man. Leonardo read something about the human body written by a man named Vitruvius. He used what Vitruvius wrote to make a drawing.

The Vitruvian Man

Leonardo also wrote about philosophy. He kept a notebook about philosophy. He wrote down some of his favorite quotes. He thought being a good person was worth more than all the money in the world.

Chapter 4: Going Back to Florence

In 1499, Leonardo left Milan. He visited a bunch of places in Italy. He made a drawing of a girl named Isabella d'Este. He didn't finish it before he left. Isabella wrote to him asking him to finish. But he never did.

Leonardo's drawing of Isabella d'Este. People still go to Paris, France to see it.

Leonardo also went to Venice. He wanted to make something that would let people breathe underwater. This was a long time before scuba diving. He then went back to Florence in April of 1500.

Leonardo was starting to get old. But he was very active. This helped him stay healthy. He was also famous in Italy because of The Last Supper. But one artist in Florence didn't want Leonardo to come back. His name was Michelangelo.

In 1500, Leonardo made a new painting of Virgin Mary and her mother, St. Anne. He didn't finish the painting.

The Virgin Mary and St. Anne

In 1502, Leonardo traveled with an army. The army was led by Cesare Borgia. He was the pope's son. Leonardo was still coming up with new weapons and plans. He made one map that looked like he was up in the air looking down at the ground. It was the first map ever made like that. It was a map of a city.

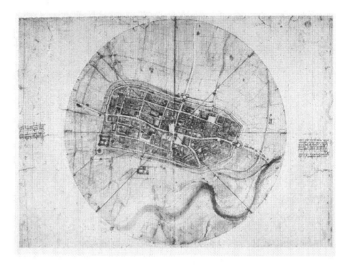

Leonardo's map of Imola

Leonardo kept making new paintings. But he was just as interested in other things. He would quit working on art to try to make new things. He may have tried to invent a flying machine in Florence. Leonardo wrote about birds and wings in his notebooks. He was trying to make something like that. People would do that in the 1890s to make gliders too.

In 1504, Florence asked Leonardo to be in charge of making a new fort. They were afraid the French would attack. The French had a lot of cannons. Leonardo needed to make a fort that could defend against cannons. The fort looked like a bunker. This made cannonballs less harmful.

Leonardo tried to make a mechanical lion in Florence too. It would take a few steps before its chest would open up. It could also move its tail and turn its head.

Around 1503, Leonardo started working on his most famous work. It's called the Mona Lisa. It's one of the most famous paintings in history. Historians think the Mona Lisa is a painting of a woman named Lisa di Anto Maria di Noldo Gherardini. She never got to have the painting.

The Mona Lisa

People still study the Mona Lisa today. She has a soft face. The woman listened to music while Leonardo drew her. This is why she has a small smile.

The Mona Lisa is a very unique painting. That's why people keep studying it. There are a lot of theories about it. Some people think the Mona Lisa was Leonardo's mother Caterina. Some people think the Mona Lisa is Leonardo himself!

The Mona Lisa's smile is the most interesting part of the painting. Some people think it looks like a smile. Other people don't. This means that people view the Mona Lisa differently. Some think she's happy and others think she's not.

Leonardo took the painting with him to France before he died. It stayed in France. Today it's in an art museum in Paris.

Chapter 5: Leonardo's Final Years

In 1506, Leonardo went back to Milan for a little bit. He made more art. But then the French king Louis XIII wanted to hire Leonardo.

In 1513, Leonardo went to Rome. He was being paid by the brother of the pope. Michelangelo was already working in Rome. So was the artist Raphael. They were making very famous paintings for the pope. But Leonardo wanted to help the army. He wasn't there to paint.

Leonardo was now 60 years old. He was still in very good shape and working hard. He kept studying a lot. He even tried to make the first solar panel. He called it a burning mirror. One legend says that he tried to put wings on a lizard to get it to fly.

In 1510, Leonardo drew a picture of himself in his notebook. He looked at himself in mirrors to draw himself. He used red chalk to make the picture.

Leonardo's drawing of himself.

Around 1514, Leonardo started to feel weaker. He couldn't paint as much anymore. He was still able to write and sketch though.

In 1516, Leonardo went to France. France had a new king, King Francis I. He only had a few people help him take the trip to France. One of them was Salai. Leonardo took everything he had to France. His house was close to where the king lived.

Leonardo didn't paint a lot in France. He wanted to study science. He kept working on mechanics. He was also making plans for everyone to read his notebooks.

Leonardo wanted to have a very nice funeral when he died. He had planned festivals in Milan. He liked to spend money and live well.

Leonardo died on May 2, 1519.

Leonardo's house and place of death in France

Chapter 6: Leonardo's Legacy

Leonardo is one of the most famous men in history. He is called the Renaissance Man. This is because he lived during the Renaissance. The Renaissance is famous because people became smarter and technology became much better. The culture in Europe changed very much because of the Renaissance. Leonardo is the best symbol of all the Renaissance's changes. He worked a lot on science. He worked on new technology. And he was a great artist. He did a lot of things better than almost everyone else.

Leonardo's drawings are almost as famous as his paintings. People still like to look at his notebooks. He tried to make flying machines. He even tried to make parachutes. Parachutes weren't made until the 1920s. And People have used his drawings to make flying machines today. Leonardo just didn't know how to build what he drew. People are still trying to make things Leonardo drew. He drew a 70 foot crossbow and even a bridge that could be carried by people.

People are still trying to figure out everything Leonardo did. Scientists use x-rays to find some of Leonardo's work. They also have Leonardo's fingerprints. This helps them find out if he worked on a painting. One of Leonardo's paintings may have been found only a few years ago. People thought it had been made in the 1800s by a German artist. But some people think it was made by Leonardo. It's called La Bella Principessa.

La Bella Principessa

Artists still study Leonardo. Michelangelo is more famous as a painter. This is probably because Leonardo was busy with other things. Leonardo never had an art workshop. He never taught other people how to paint either. That meant fewer people made art like he did.

Leonardo was way ahead of his time. People in the 1500s weren't thinking a lot about flying or science. This meant they didn't understand a lot of his work. They didn't pay a lot of attention to that stuff in the notebooks. But today, we know that Leonardo was a genius. It would take 300-

400 years for people to bring Leonardo's ideas to life. Things like helicopters, tanks, and calculators were made in the 1900s. But Leonardo was the first to think of them in the 1500s. The world just wasn't ready for Leonardo in his own lifetime.

Made in United States
Orlando, FL
07 February 2022

14568686R00024